b) Responses will vary. E
   than general. For exam
   treatment and it got m(

9. a) This one verse would a   ...ders that John is one with them, that he, like them, is being punished for his belief in Jesus.

  b) To John, the three words capture what it means to participate in the Christian life. Additional question: How does this same understanding apply today?

10. These churches are found in the major cities of Asia Minor.

11. While much of John's imagery here comes from the writings of Daniel and Ezekiel, there are numerous images that reinforce God's presence among the people of Israel (e.g., on the mountain with Moses, leading the former slaves by a pillar of cloud and a pillar of fire, in all possible hiding places).

12. John's readers believed that the power to act resided in the hands and feet and that a person's will, intellect, and judgment resided in the eyes and heart. His vision describes a powerful, just being.

13. Responses will vary.

14. a) The two-edged sword symbolizes judgment at the end-time. In this case, the heavenly being's words are judgment, declaring both good and evil.

  b) Responses will vary. People may share times God's Word has brought them peace as well as times when God's Word has pointed out their failings.

15. a) Those persecuted for their faith can hold out hope because Jesus is the Lord of life and death and the judge of all.

  b) Responses will vary. It is early in the study; people may or may not be willing to share personal stories.

16. The guardian spirits of the seven churches. As he holds the seven stars in his hand, the risen Christ continues to guard the churches.

17. Answers will vary. It is important for people to recognize the use of symbolism and understand Revelation as a book of consolation and hope.

LESSON 2

Revelation 2–3

1. Answers will vary. Some people may mention what they learned about apocalyptic literature or about the symbolism found there. Each week, the first question will allow participants to review the previous lesson before moving forward.

2. Ephesus may have been the first church to be addressed because: It was an important commercial center at the mouth of the river Cayster and among the largest cities of the province. There was a substantial Jewish population in Ephesus. Paul used Ephesus for his base of operations for two years. The author of John's Gospel is associated with Ephesus. Mary, the mother of Jesus, may have died there. Ephesus was the home of many shrines to Greek deities and imperial cult temples, including Artemis, goddess of fertility.

3. a) Ephesian Christians were known for their good works, endurance, intolerance of wickedness, the ability to discern imposters, their suffering, and their vitality.

   b) Responses will vary. Encourage group members to give specific examples of behaviors that show endurance, tolerance, etc.

4. a) They have lost the love they once had.

   b) Christians are being persecuted; Greek and Roman pagan influences surround the Ephesians; it is difficult to stand up against all these temptations.

5. Those who will be allowed to eat of the tree of life are being restored to an ultimate relationship with God such as Adam and Eve enjoyed in Paradise. Also, the Ephesians were devoted to Artemis, the goddess of fertility, a poor substitute for the "tree of life."

6. a) Throughout the Scriptures, those who are poor are God's special possessions. Those in Smyrna are rich because God is on their side, even when they suffer.

ANSWER GUIDE

REVELATION

LITTLE ROCK SCRIPTURE STUDY

*A ministry of the Diocese of Little Rock
in partnership with Liturgical Press*

LESSON 1

Revelation 1

1. Responses will vary and may include common misconceptions. Allow group members to become consciously aware of their perceptions, which may change and expand in future weeks.

2. a) Apocalyptic literature consoles people in situations of persecution, interprets historical events in light of God's sovereignty and the triumph of good over evil, and persuades people to remain faithful to covenant.

   b) Responses will vary. Some may believe that apocalyptic writing predicts the end of the world, etc.

3. a) The author's exact identity is unknown. We know that the author was an early Jewish Christian prophet by the name of John.

   b) The text provides few clues, but Revelation probably was written between AD 95 and 96.

   c) The audience was Christians in the churches of Asia Minor, around the time of persecutions by the emperor Domitian.

4. Apocalypse comes from a Greek word meaning "revelation." The visions and voices pertain to heavenly things and future events.

5. The revelation is "to show . . . what must happen soon."

6. The message is not prophetic because it predicts distant future events. It is prophetic because, like the prophets before him, John is acting as a spokesperson for God and calling people to conversion.

7. Each person's choice will depend on his or her religious training and personal experiences. For example, a person who has recently lost a loved one might connect most with the title, "firstborn of the dead," etc.

8. a) John is reassuring his readers that Jesus has conquered death and sin through his life, death, and resurrection. In a dark and frightening time, John wants his readers to remain confident that God is sovereign and that God's love will prevail.

b) Responses will vary. Encourage some of the group to mention someone close to them, rather than well-known public figures.

7. a) Conflicts between Christians and non-Christians, rich and poor, between local and provincial governments, etc.

   b) Christians live in a world filled with conflicts. Try to focus discussion on how our Christianity affects the way we react and respond to conflicts.

8. a) Buying and eating meat sacrificed to idols occurs in both cities.

   b) This practice compromises the faith and could confuse or scandalize new believers. In a broader sense, John is scolding his readers for letting the influences of the wider culture compromise the integrity of their Christianity.

9. This is an opportunity for self-evaluation, a time to identify strengths and weaknesses.

10. Responses will vary. Encourage people to share the reasons for their responses.

11. Discussion will vary depending on experiences. People may recognize that a parish can offer lots of activities, while excluding certain groups of people. A parish may have beautiful facilities but no outreach to the poor or no real sense of community, etc.

12. White symbolizes the purity of baptism, immortality, resurrection, etc. Use of the color white is another way John holds out hope and consolation to his readers.

13. a) The Key of David symbolizes Jesus' authority and suggests that their belief in the Messiah gives them authority as well.

    b) Responses will vary. People may talk about both obvious and subtle opportunities for growth and change in their relationship with God.

14. By the time water reached Laodicea from the hot springs in nearby Hierapolis, it was lukewarm. Help the group realize that both negative and positive things can distract us and make us complacent.

15. Discussion. Suffering itself is not necessarily redemptive, but the way we respond to suffering can make it redemptive.
16. Responses will vary. Help ensure that opinions expressed are accepted and not criticized.
17. Ample examples can be found for the three goals, which are: to console the audience, to assure the audience that God is sovereign and that goodness will prevail, and to call the audience to conversion.

LESSON 3

Revelation 4–7

1. Ancient Christian communities, surrounded by paganism and faced with persecution, struggled to remain faithful, to resist being influenced by idols of all kinds, to maintain their identity, to remain loving—the same struggles we face today.
2. a) A theophany, like the one in 4:1-11, is a manifestation of God.
   b) Typical theophanies include a mountain setting, heavenly voices, fire, lightning, and thunder. The seer is taken to see where God resides and often is in a trance.
3. The holiness of God comes through loud and clear in the calls of Moses and Isaiah, in the prayers of Israel, in the experiences of those who encountered Jesus, and in numerous other ways.
4. a) Titles include "lion of the tribe of Judah" and "root of David."
   b) Other messianic titles include son of David, son of Abraham (Matt 1:1); root of Jesse (Isa 11:1); Holy One of God (Mark 1:24).
5. Three actions made him worthy: he was slaughtered, he ransomed the holy ones, and he made them a kingdom and priests for God.
6. The whole scene depicts triumph, praise, and trust in Jesus, who stands ready to dispense justice. Though John's readers may be oppressed, they have power and kingship through Jesus. The Lamb, though slain, achieves victory.

7. a) Conquest, war, famine, and death are their powers.

   b) Encourage acceptance of various opinions, as group members will base their answers on personal experience, upbringing, culture, etc.

8. Chances are good that group members will have lived through at least one of the U.S. conflicts of the 20th and 21st centuries. Discussion may include divorce, mental illness, post traumatic stress, chronic pain, forced immigration, etc.

9. Though not martyrs, all of us are called to bear witness to God's Word. Examples are endless and may include changed attitudes, kind and reconciling words or actions, improved family interaction, more tolerance, giving up control and striving to let God lead, serving those in need, etc.

10. a) These signs include earthquakes, the sun turning black, the moon turning to blood, etc. The people are terrified.

    b) The intense cosmic activity suggests hope because all of creation is working on God's behalf.

11. The tone shifts immediately in verse 1 as four protective angels give reason for hope.

12. In the Greco-Roman world, "branding" indicated ownership of slaves. In this symbolic context, those with the seal are set apart as belonging to God, under God's protection, and therefore, exempt from God's wrath.

13. God marked Cain to protect him. The Israelites were protected with the mark of blood on their doors during the final plague in Egypt. Those who were saddened over the sin in Jerusalem were marked with an "X" on their foreheads and were thus protected.

14. a) John's readers would have understood the number symbolically as perfection or fullness, multiplied to include a massive crowd of people, but not as a literal count.

    b) Understood literally, this might make us believe that Christ will save only a certain small number of people. In contrast, John means to show Christ as wanting to save as many as we could imagine.

15. These items symbolize victory, especially victory in war.

16. Because Jesus (the Lamb) offers the perfect sacrifice of his life, his blood has the power to purify us from sinfulness.
17. Allow people to discuss how they were affected by this profound message of hope.

LESSON 4

Revelation 8–11

1. Allow people to discuss their reactions to the dramatic, fantastic apocalyptic images they are encountering.
2. Responses will vary. Some people may struggle to find silence for prayer. Others may be very uncomfortable with silence.
3. a) The hail and fire (8:7) remind us of the seventh plague; the tainting of the water (8:9-10) recalls the first plague; and darkness is similar to the ninth plague.

    b) They are miracles because they are part of God's larger plan for the salvation of Christians.
4. "One-third" tells readers that the destruction is limited in scope, sending a message of warning—the final judgment is yet to come.
5. Both use the image of horses ready for battle. Both probably symbolize the Parthians, long-standing enemies of the Romans.
6. Here, and throughout apocalyptic literature, passive verbs are used to describe activity (e.g., locusts *were given* power). This very form suggests that, despite appearances, God controls the course of history, allows things to happen, and will ultimately triumph.
7. Responses will vary. It is good for people to identify ways that they regularly demonstrate their Christianity.
8. The description of the locusts is highly imaginative, even fantastic. If we take it literally, we would believe that a science fiction event will usher in the end of time. John's real message is that cultural evils of our own time cause immense human suffering.

9. Responses will vary and may include stubbornness, laziness, anger and resentment, disillusionment, preoccupation with other "gods," etc.

10. Responses will vary. This is a good chance to emphasize that God does not cause evil and suffering.

11. a) Responses will vary and may include: sports and movie stars, youth and vitality, money and possessions, fashion and status, etc.

    b) Responses may include the above as well as many others. Anything that we base our security on can become an idol: work, study, food, alcohol, drugs, even another human being.

12. Their prophecy would have included calling people to repentance as well as announcing suffering for their people. It's never easy to speak a difficult truth.

13. a) The two witnesses, called olive trees and lamp stands, recall the anointed King Zerubbabel and high priest Joshua in Zechariah 4:12. They built the temple and stand by to serve the Lord.

    b) The two witnesses could also represent Moses and Elijah.

14. 11:7-13 follows the pattern of classic Old Testament Wisdom literature. Its message is one of consolation and hope: God is sovereign over all things, a just judge who will rescue the righteous and punish the wicked, and a merciful creator who will not destroy creation forever.

15. The symbolic names of Sodom and Egypt represent immorality. The use of the names is a warning to the "great city" of Rome.

16. a) Jeremiah is said to have hidden the ark in a cave.

    b) John's vision signifies God's protective presence.

17. a) Fear motivates worship in 11:13. In 11:15-18, God's authority and kingship lead the elders to praise and worship.

    b) Responses will vary and should help people get in touch with their dependence on God.

LESSON 5

Revelation 12–14

1. This is a good time to affirm that others' insights can help us understand God's Word.
2. The birth of a male child is a sign of God's blessing; the child is destined to rule with great strength; God makes a place of protection for the woman in the desert; the child is rescued from the dragon and given to God.
3. In the desert, Israel encountered God, entered into covenant, and felt God's sustaining presence. The desert symbolizes God's continuing presence with those who are in trouble.
4. The woman could represent Eve, a redeemed Israel, Mary the mother of Jesus, or even the church.
5. It symbolizes the ultimate battle between good and evil, between Christ and Satan, won by Christ through his death and resurrection.
6. a) "Ancient serpent" refers to the snake who seduced Eve; "Devil" means slanderer or enemy; "Satan" means accuser in Hebrew; "deceiver of the whole world" speaks for itself.

    b) Responses will vary. Encourage people to talk about everyday victories over gossip, lying, prejudice, verbal abuse, temptations of alcohol, drugs, cigarettes, over-eating, over-speaking, etc. Additional question: With what do you fight these?
7. Verses 1 and 5: "blasphemous names" refers to assigning titles such as Lord and God to Roman emperors. Verse 2: the three creatures symbolize Rome and two other empires. Verse 3: "the wound" refers to Nero. Verse 4 is probably a reference to the emperor cult. Verse 5 refers to Rome's offenses against God and the Christians who worship God.
8. Responses will vary. In our modern, affluent culture, many things capture our imagination, energy, and time, often leaving us worn out and empty, or stressed or confused, etc.
9. It is half of seven (a symbolic number meaning fullness). It refers to a limited time of suffering.

10. a) It speaks like the dragon (11:13) and, like the first beast, received its authority from the dragon. It has horns like the dragon and the voice of the dragon.

   b) This beast probably symbolizes the Roman emperor since this second beast is doing the bidding of the first beast, the Roman Empire.

11. They are references to emperor worship, including venerating the emperor's image; to the practice of imprinting the emperor's image on coins needed for commerce; and to manipulating the images or statues to make them "speak," requiring people to offer sacrifices to the emperor, etc.

12. a) It was somewhat common to assign numbers to letters of a word or a name and use the resulting numbers as a "label." Since 666 is the numerical value of the letters in Nero's name, the beast most likely refers to Nero.

    b) Responses will vary.

13. Literally, the vision could represent soldiers in a holy war who abstained from sexual activity, or celibate priests in the heavenly liturgy. Figuratively, their virginity symbolizes faithfulness to God/Christ and refusal to engage in cult worship.

14. Responses will vary.

15. Because Babylon conquered Jerusalem, destroyed the Temple, and sent Israel into exile, it became a symbol of all forces opposed to God. John is saying that Rome should be judged for seducing God's people.

16. a) Good works will be rewarded.

    b) Never-ending torment in burning sulfur might encourage repentance!

17. Discuss how the Bible offers countless images or depictions of God, all of them inadequate but helpful reminders that God is beyond any limited definitions. In this case, love recognizes and abhors injustice; those persecuted need to remember that God is with them.

18. It is a traditional metaphor for ultimate judgment and answers the question posed in 6:10: "How long will it be . . . before you sit in judgment?"

LESSON 6

Revelation 15–18

1. Responses will vary.
2. All three focus on God's greatness and the power to save.
3. The tent of testimony is an allusion to the tent of meeting in Exodus. The seven angels are like the priests of the Temple.
4. a) Plagues are not gratuitous violence but a call to repentance and to worship God alone.

   b) The passage recalls the seven plagues of Egypt, sent by God to make Pharaoh repent.
5. a) The "works" here refer to participation in activities that support the deceiver, Rome: politics, commerce, cultic practices, etc.

   b) Responses will vary. The fear of facing our struggles (and the part we have played in them) can be extremely painful.
6. John's readers would have been familiar with Jesus' words (Matt 24:44) and Paul's teaching (1 Thess 5:2) and with Jesus' gentle love. The reference ought to discourage us from trying to calculate when the end will come. It ought to encourage us to live prepared, expectant and joyful lives.
7. The Hebrew word means "Mountain of Megiddo." Megiddo, strategically located between Mount Carmel and the Jordan River, was the entryway for invading armies and the site of fierce battles in Israel's history. To John, it symbolizes the ultimate and last battle.
8. Prostitution and adultery were common metaphors for idol worship, material excess, corruption, emperor worship, etc.
9. Spend some time talking about the need to recognize signs of God's direction in everyday life. God may indeed grab our attention through prayer or Scripture reading, but also through conversations with others, crises, family struggles, the beauty of nature, etc.

10. The passage symbolically describes evil and corruption in the Roman Empire. But God uses evil to destroy evil and is victorious in the end.
11. All kinds of examples may surface: corrupt business practices causing a business to fail, an unjust supervisor ending up being fired, etc. You may also choose to discuss people's reactions when these things have happened. Were they able to be compassionate?
12. Discussion. Try to focus on attitudes that drive behaviors: fear vs. trust; acceptance vs. judgment, etc.
13. Babylon is an evil place (welcomes demons and unclean spirits); it exhibits lawless passion and a "drive for luxury."
14. Responses will vary and may include political, corporate, and personal greed and corruption; an increase in addictions; the widening gap between rich and poor, etc. Help the group look critically at moral decay in our own culture and the Christian's call to action.
15. Responses may include spiritual and biblical reading, regular prayer, ending the day with an examination of conscience, etc.
16. Responses may include feelings of discomfort, fear, confusion, etc. Focus on the group's reactions to the vengeance. Our reactions often give clues about what God wants us to hear.
17. They will lose money; they realize their guilt, and fear they will face the same fate.
18. Some people may feel comfortable enough to share personal experiences with this saying.

LESSON 7

Revelation 19–22

1. Responses will vary.
2. The bride symbolizes the church, rejoicing because the time of God's vindication has come. The marriage symbolizes the final victory in heaven, the final coming of God's kingdom.

3. In Old Testament usage, the word means "praise Yahweh," appropriate for this song of victory.
4. Even when we are blessed with good teachers, pastors, and prophets, we must focus on developing our personal relationship with God, not on human personalities.
5. Responses will vary. Try to center on how the titles affect or encourage prayer.
6. The wedding feast is a joyous reunion of the righteous, the coming of the kingdom, the victory. "God's great feast" in 19:17-18 describes the annihilation of God's enemies with gruesome imagery. It is the judgment, the crushing of the wicked.
7. Discussion will give one last reminder of how to read the book of Revelation.
8. One thousand years represents the time after Jesus Christ died and rose, but before the final judgment.
9. The passage shows the martyred faithful on the judgment seat. They have been rewarded for their righteousness. The message should bring comfort and hope, even in the present persecution.
10. a) John is referring to Ezekiel 38, a prophecy of Gog's brutal destruction. All references are reminders of pagan nations who at one time tried to destroy God's people.

    b) Once again, John is trying to tell his readers that God will destroy the wicked all over the world.
11. Some, but not all, believed in a general resurrection of the dead at the end of time.
12. Responses will vary. We all do good and noble things. Encourage people to acknowledge that fact in themselves.
13. Isaiah used bridal imagery to describe the restoration of Jerusalem. Ezekiel used covenant imagery and spoke of God dwelling with humans. Isaiah talks about the absence of suffering and death. Other traditional Old Testament images include the water of life.
14. Its cubic shape recalls the holy of holies in Solomon's Temple. It has three gates on each of four walls, like Ezekiel's plan of

the Temple. It has 12 precious stones, recalling the high priests' breastplate and representing the twelve tribes.

15. There is no need for the mediation that the Temple formerly provided. God and the Lamb reside directly, their power and radiance providing the city's light.

16. a) It does not mean that evil people will always be evil. More likely, it is meant as a warning against complacency.

    b) Responses will vary.

17. a) Responses will vary. Being aware of thirst often precedes spiritual growth.

    b) Responses will vary and may include prayer, Scripture, sacraments, nature, family, friends, service work, reading, writing, etc.

18. Personal responses will vary. Our baptism calls us to bring about God's kingdom on earth, even as we await its perfection in the final coming.

LITTLE ROCK SCRIPTURE STUDY
Little Rock, Arkansas

LITURGICAL PRESS
Collegeville, Minnesota

© 2007 by Little Rock Scripture Study,
Little Rock, Arkansas.